JAKE SHIMABUKURO

THE GREATEST DAY

Music transcriptions by Pete Billmann

ISBN 978-1-5400-3746-6

HAL•LEONARD®

Visit Hal Leonard Online at
www.halleonard.com

Contact Us:
Hal Leonard
7777 West Bluemound Road
Milwaukee, WI 53213
Email: info@halleonard.com

In Europe contact:
Hal Leonard Europe Limited
42 Wigmore Street
Marylebone, London, W1U 2RN
Email: info@halleonardeurope.com

In Australia contact:
Hal Leonard Australia Pty. Ltd.
4 Lentara Court
Cheltenham, Victoria, 3192 Australia
Email: info@halleonard.com.au

Time of the Season

Lyric and Music by Rod Argent

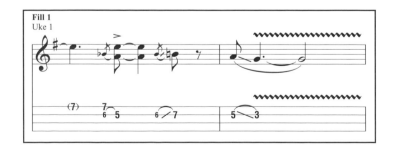

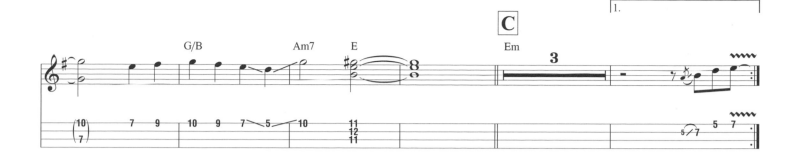

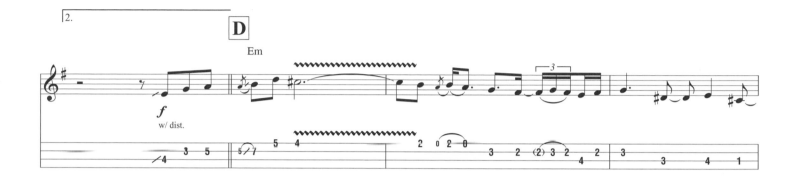

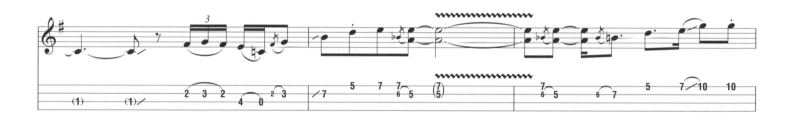

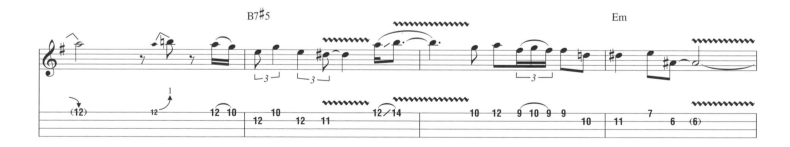

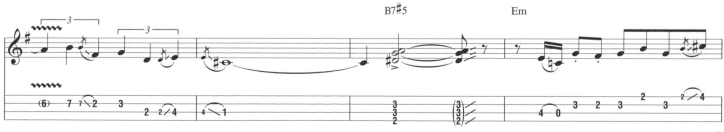

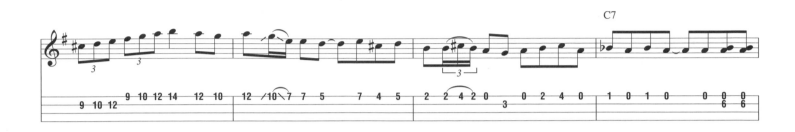

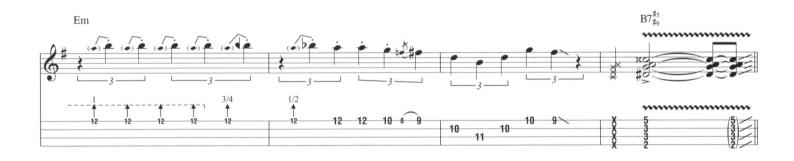

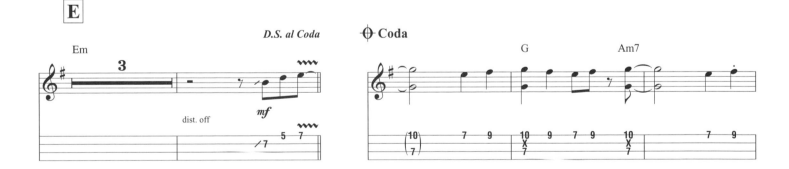

E

D.S. al Coda   Coda

The Greatest Day

Written by Jake Shimabukuro

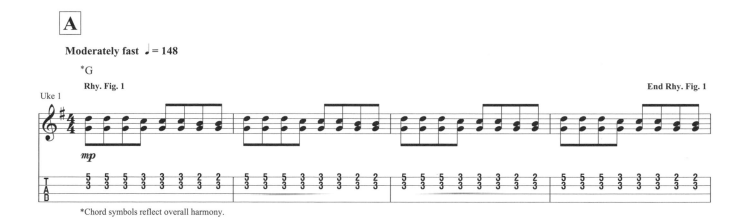

*Chord symbols reflect overall harmony.

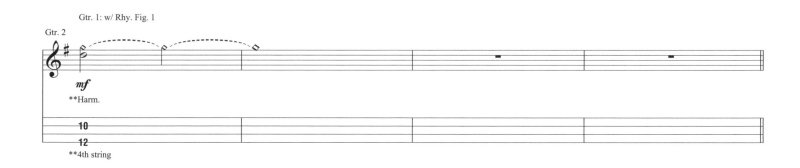

**4th string

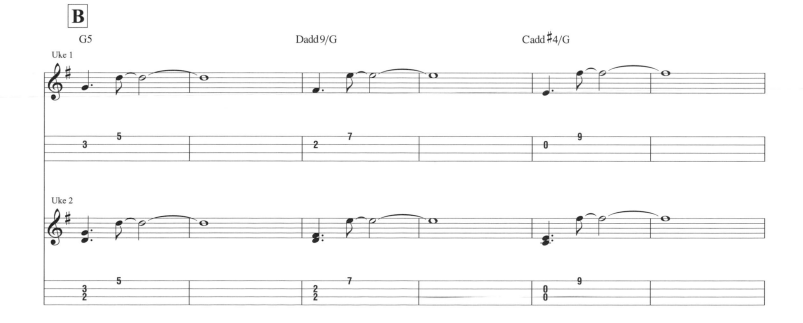

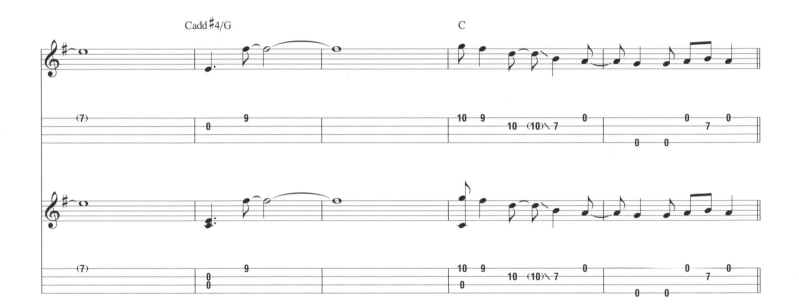

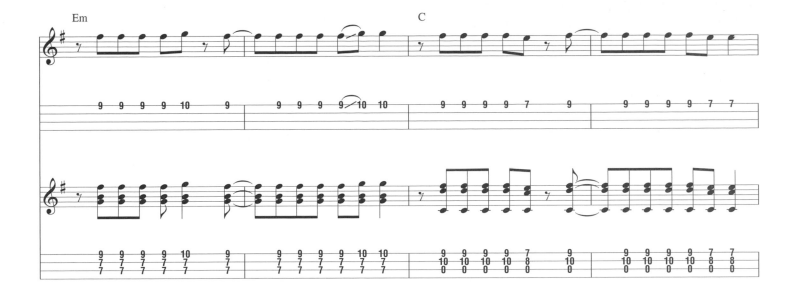

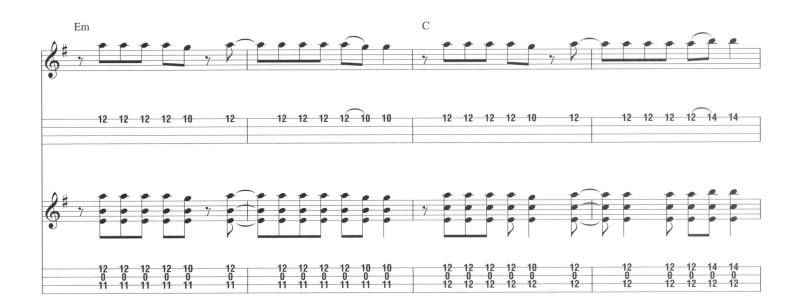

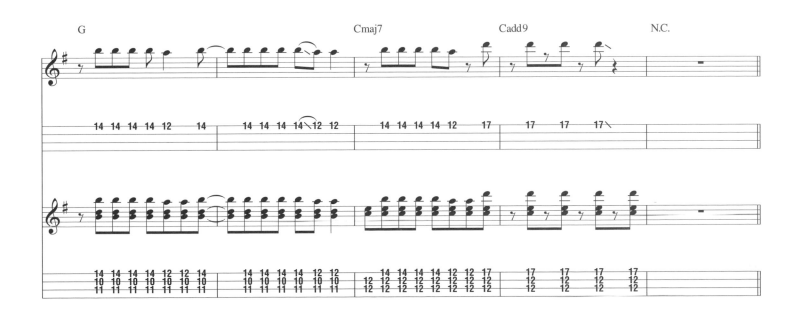

D

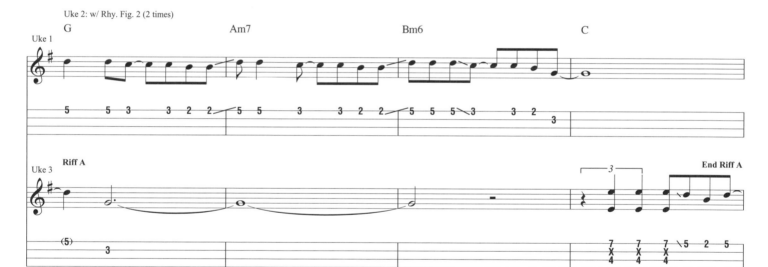

To Coda

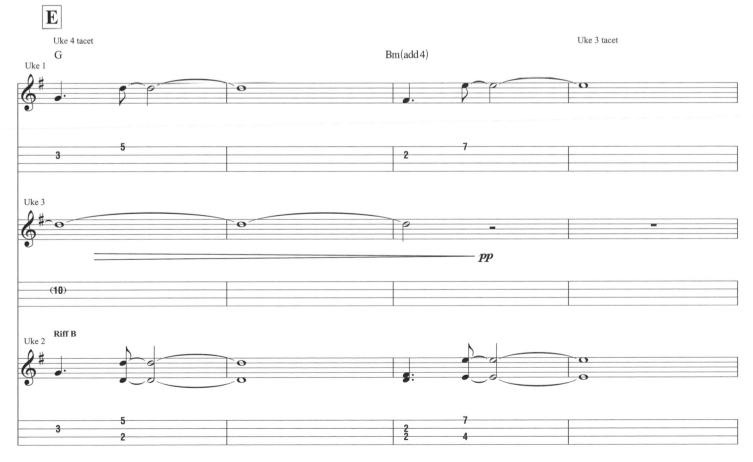

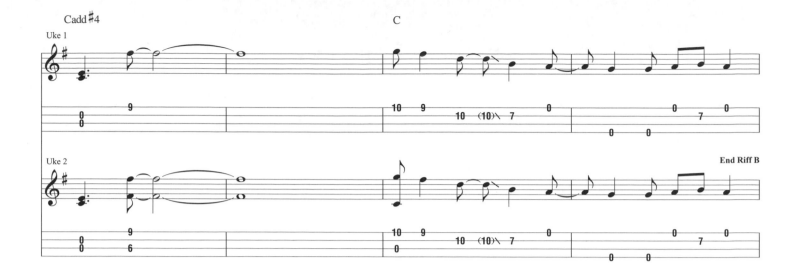

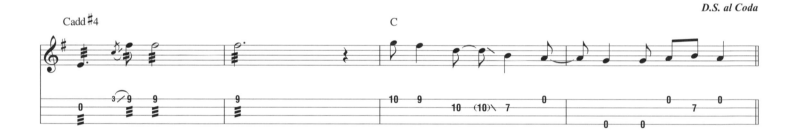

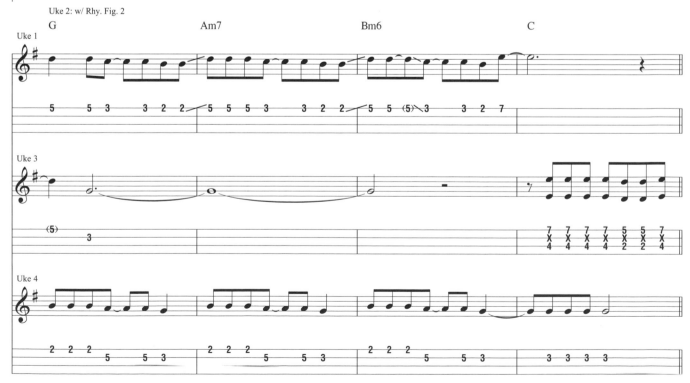

F

Uke 2: w/ Rhy. Fig. 2 (3 times)
Ukes 3 & 4 tacet

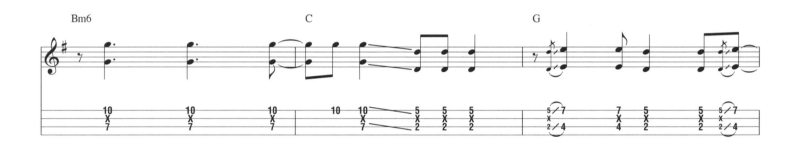

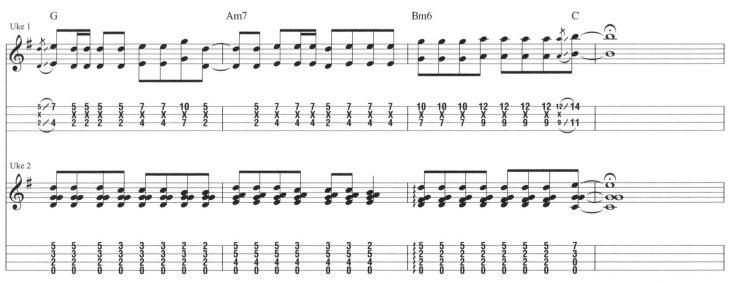

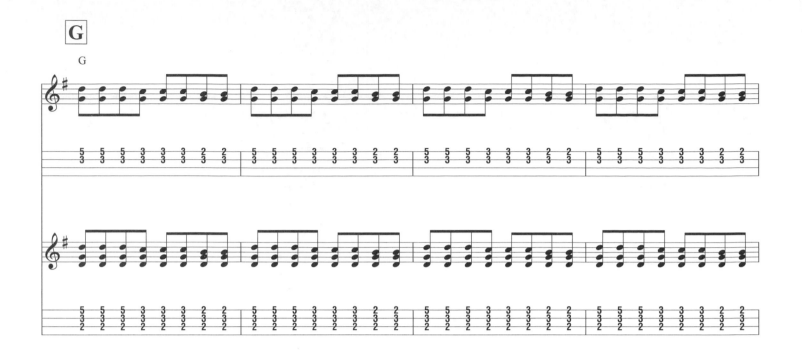

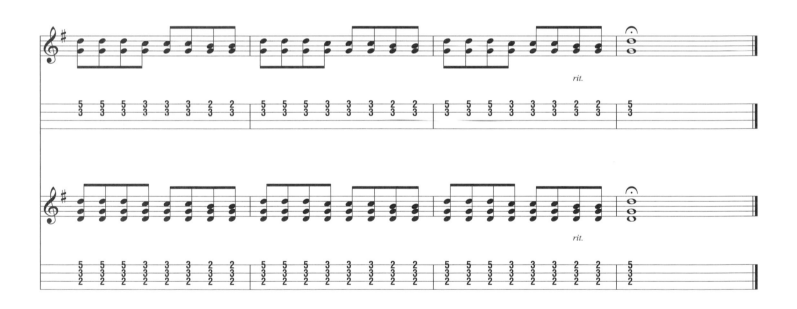

Eleanor Rigby

Words and Music by John Lennon and Paul McCartney

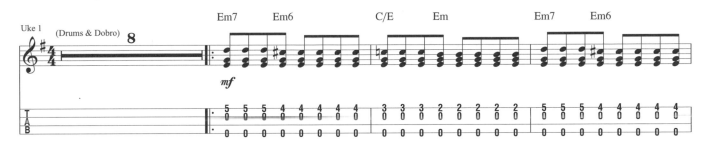

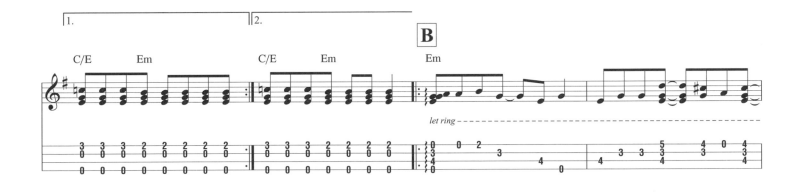

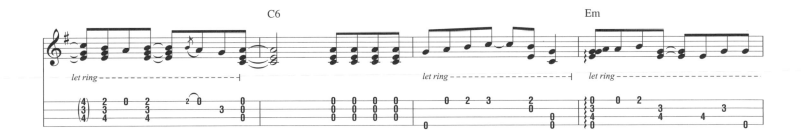

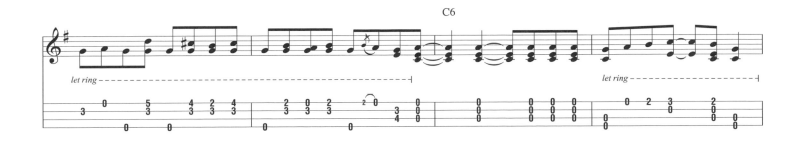

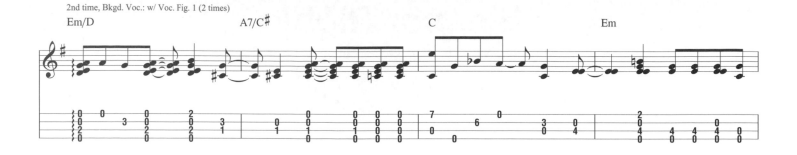

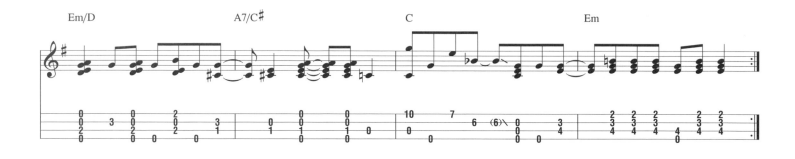

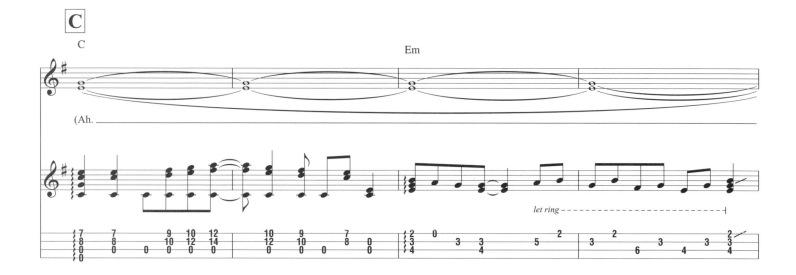

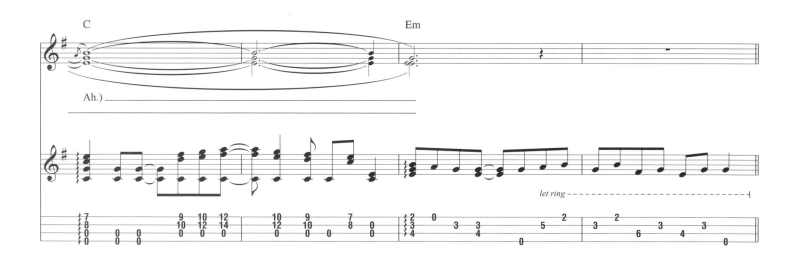

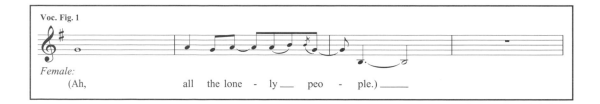

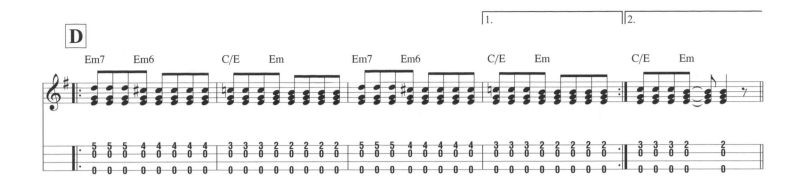

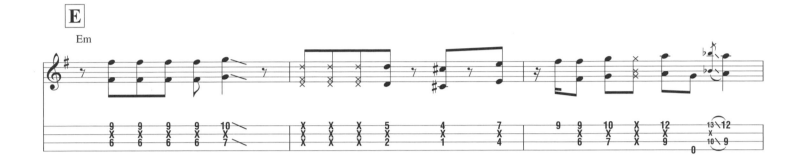

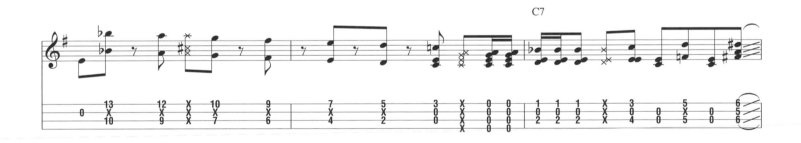

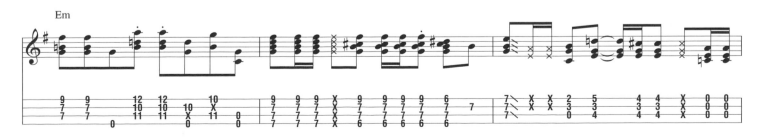

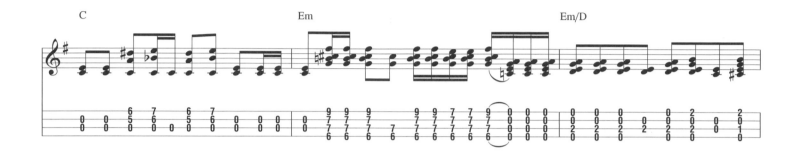

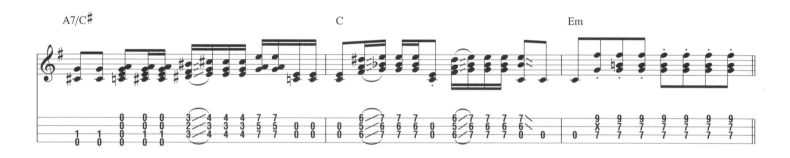

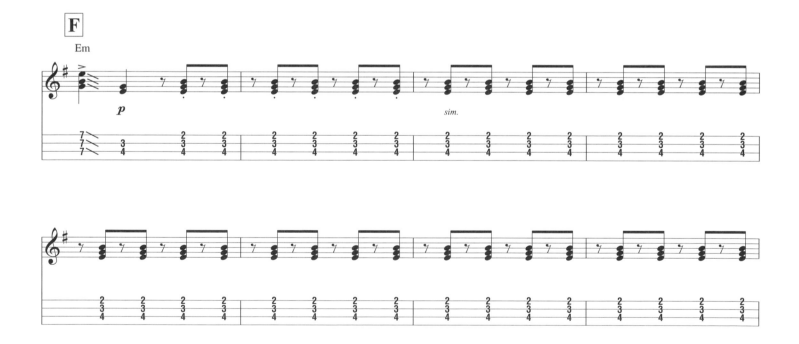

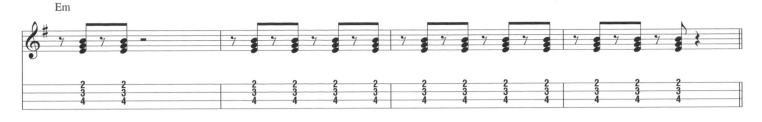

(Ah, all the lone - ly____ peo - ple.) ____

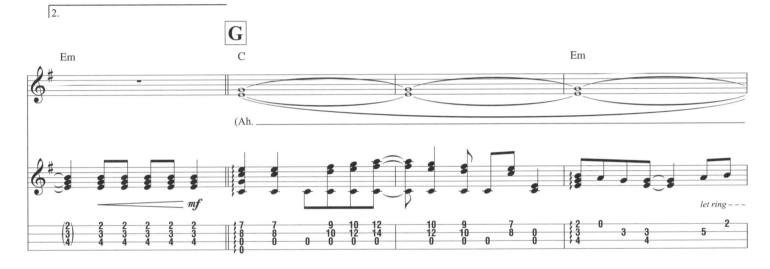

(Ah.

Ah.

Ah.)

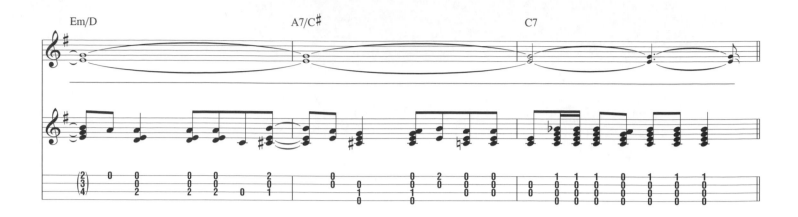

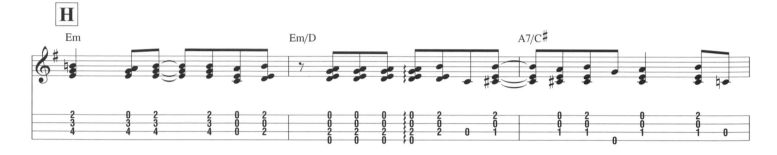

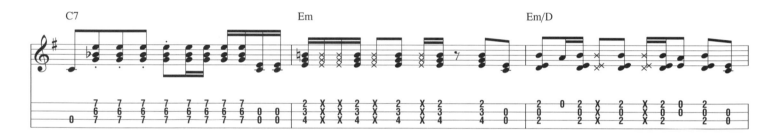

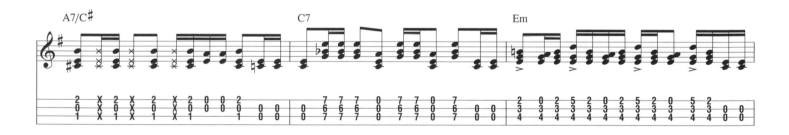

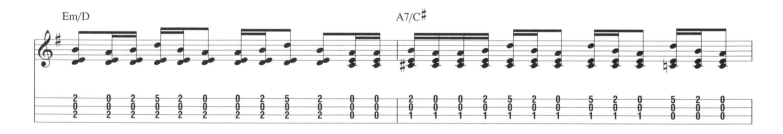

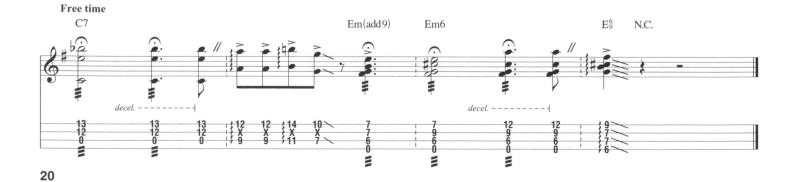

Pangram

Written by Jake Shimabukuro and Nolan Verner

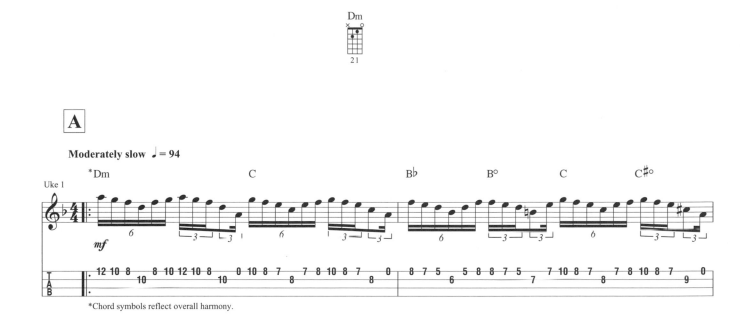

Chord symbols reflect overall harmony.

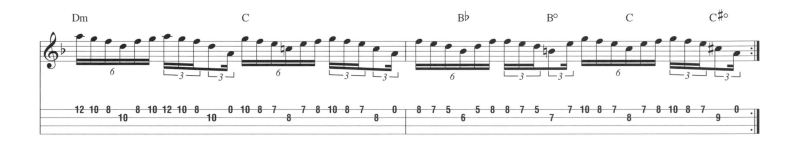

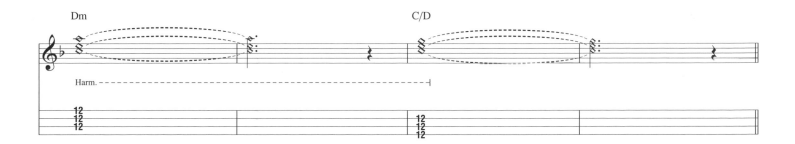

B

*See top of first page of song for chord diagrams pertaining to rhythm slashes.

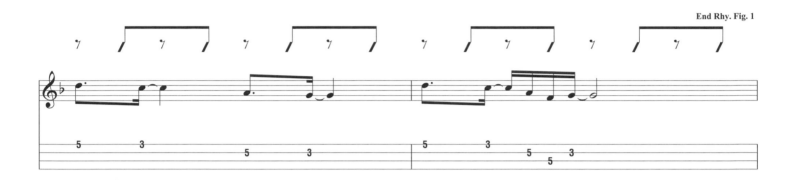

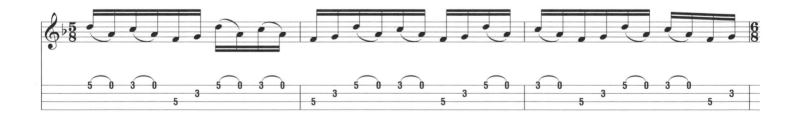

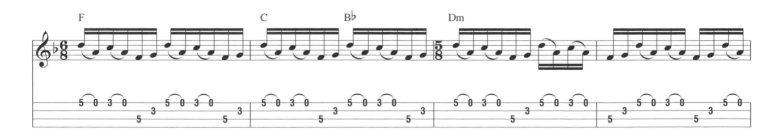

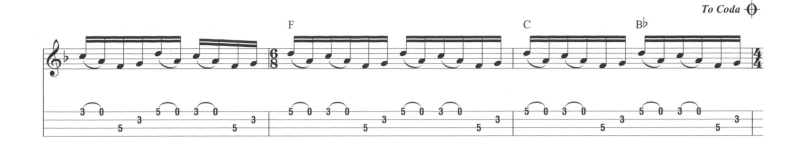

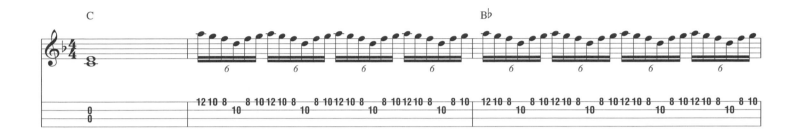

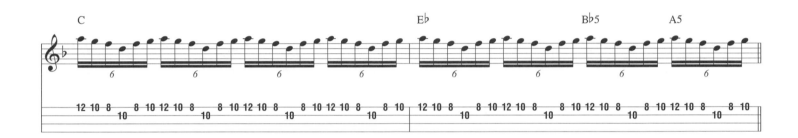

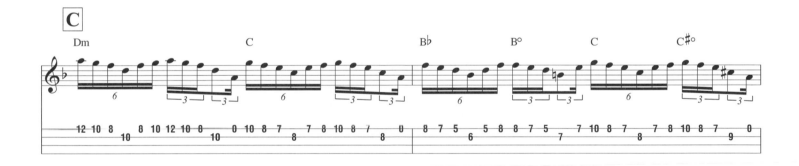

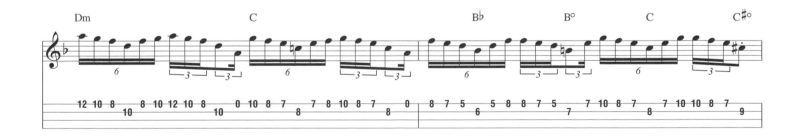

D.S. al Coda

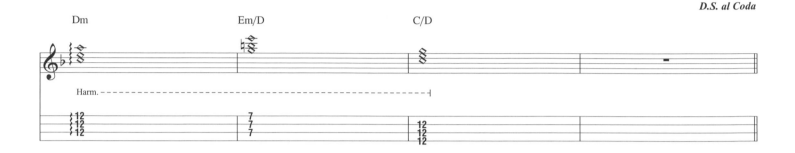

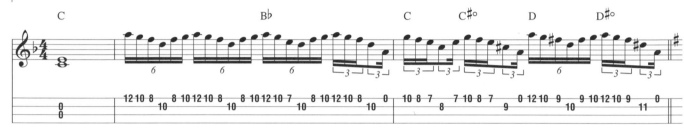

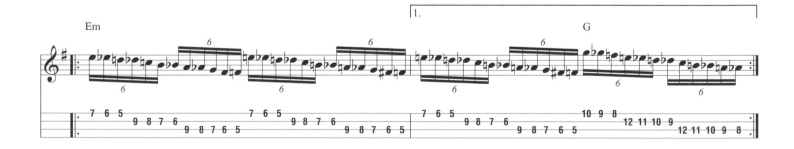

D

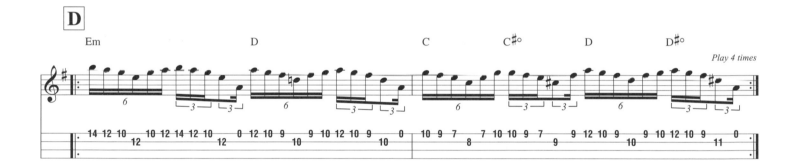

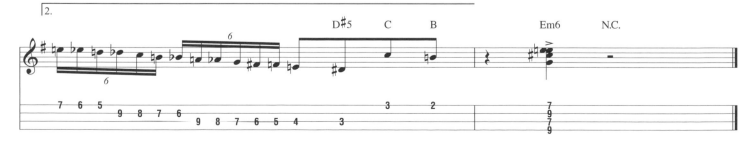

Bizarre Love Triangle

Words and Music by Gilliam Gilbert, Peter Hood, Stephen Morris and Bernard Sumner

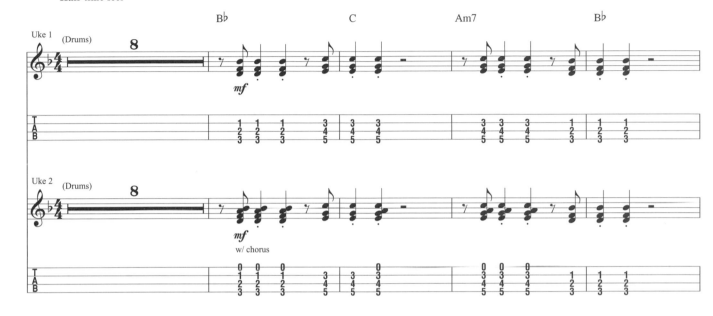

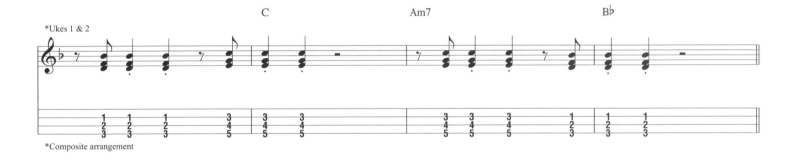

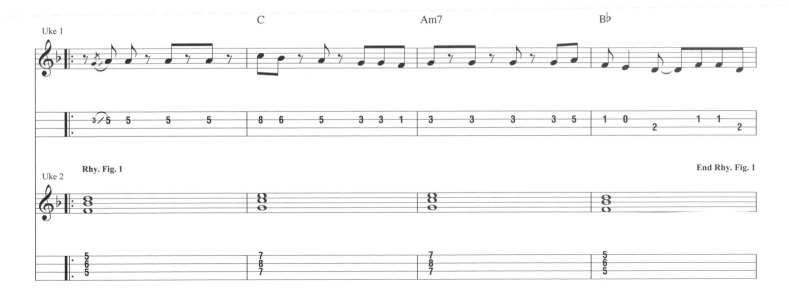

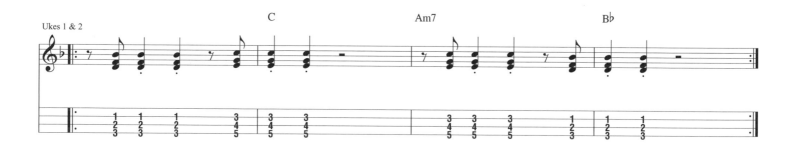

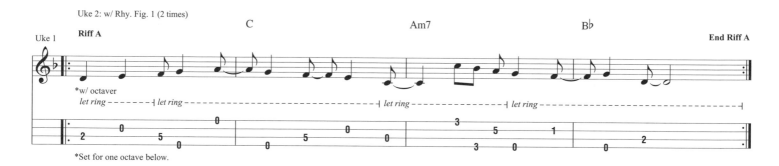

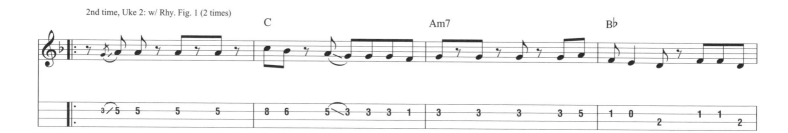

Chorus

Uke 1: w/ Riff A (4 times)

Female:(Oo, _____ fall - in'. _____

Find the _____ mo - ment. _____

Uke 2: w/ Rhy. Fig. 1 (2 times)

Fall - in'. _____

Find the _____ mo - ment.)

(Oo.) _____

Interlude

Uke 2

Harm.

Verse

Uke 1: w/ Riff A (4 times)
Uke 2: w/ Rhy. Fig. 1 (4 times)

1., 2. Ev - 'ry time I see _____ you fall - in', I get down on my knees _____ and pray. _____

Wait - ing for that fi - nal mo - ment, you say the words that I _____ can't say. _____

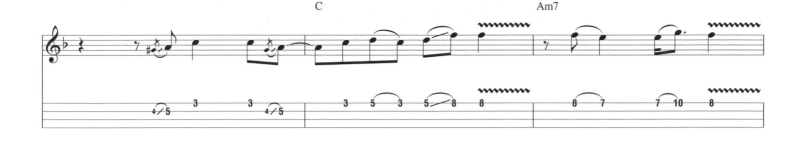

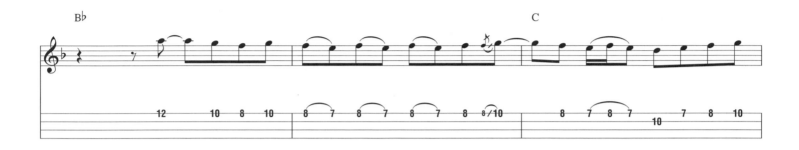

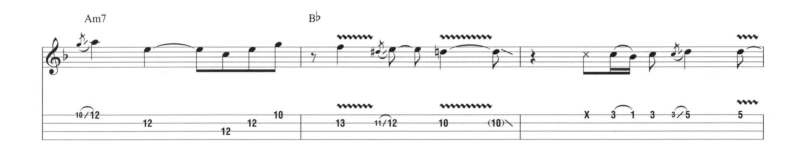

Outro

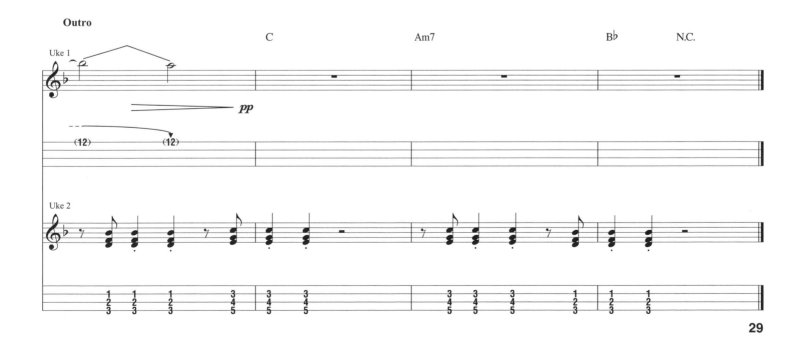

Straight A's

Written by Jake Shimabukuro and Nolan Verner

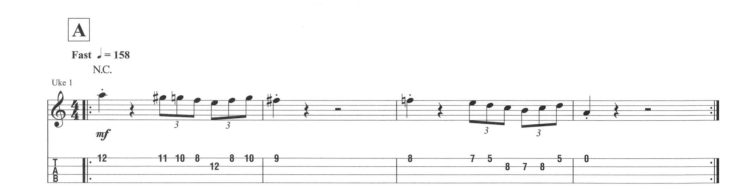

*Chord symbols reflect implied harmony.

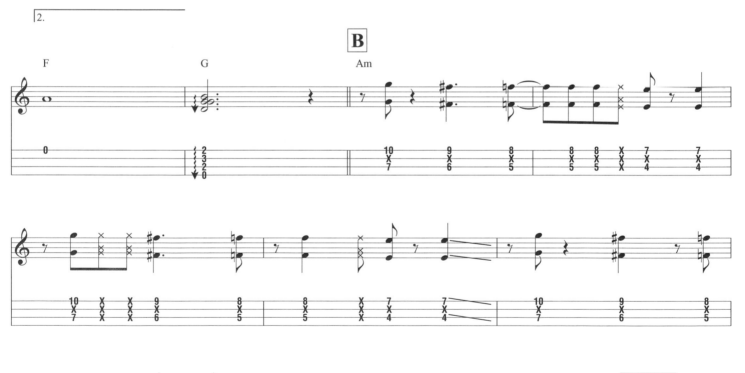

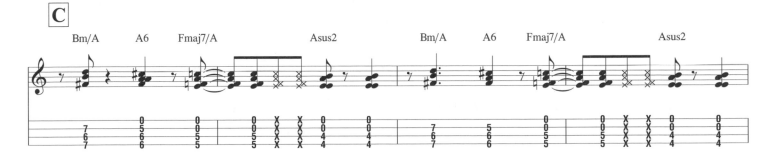

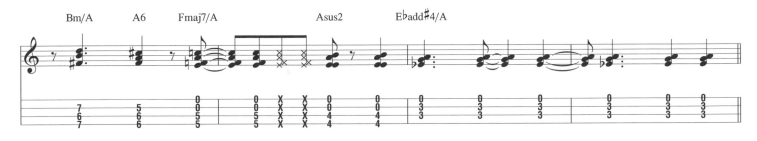

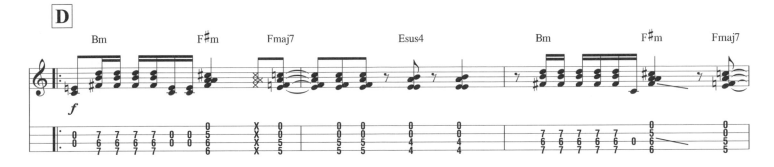

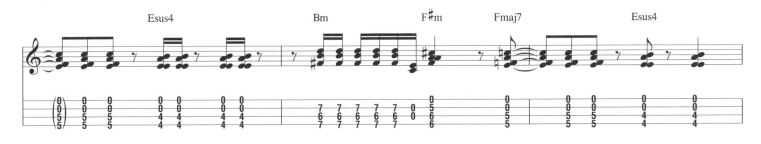

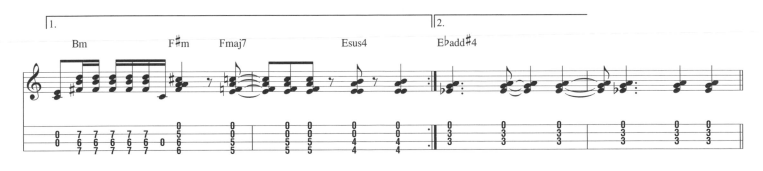

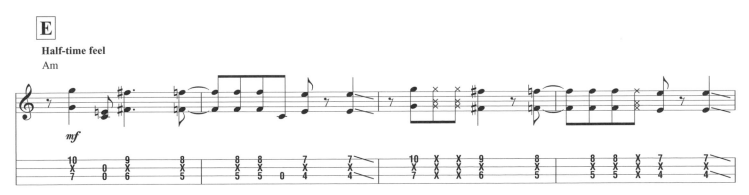

End half-time feel

F

Am

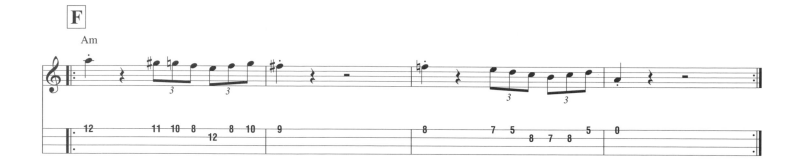

N.C.

Bm   F#m   Fmaj7   Esus4   E♭add#4

Play 3 times

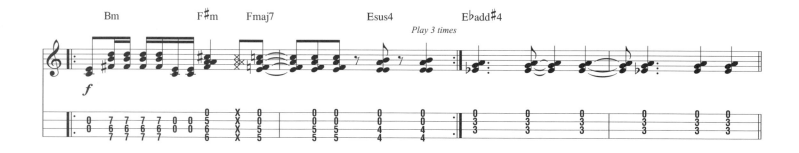

G

Dsus2

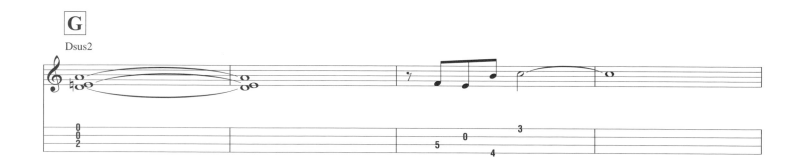

Uke 1 tacet

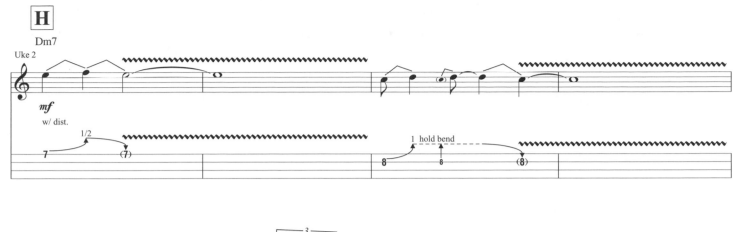

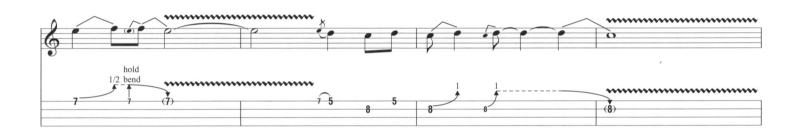

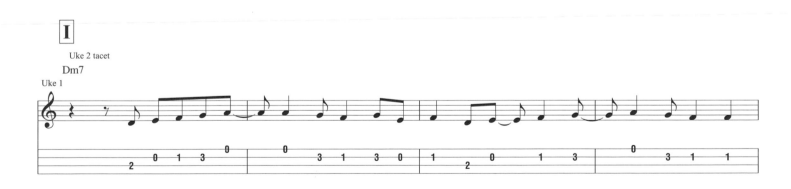

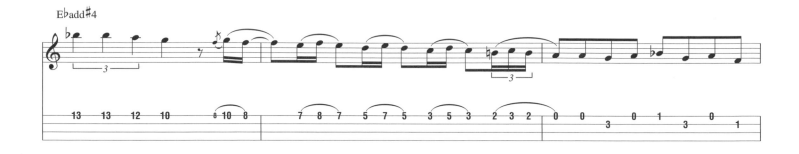

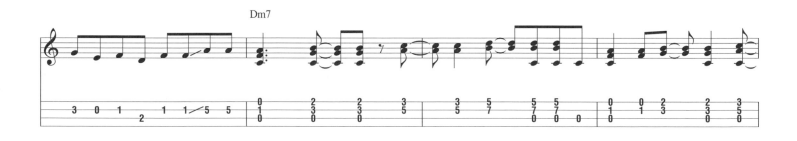

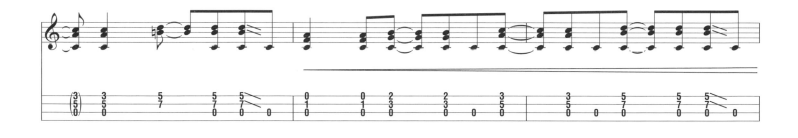

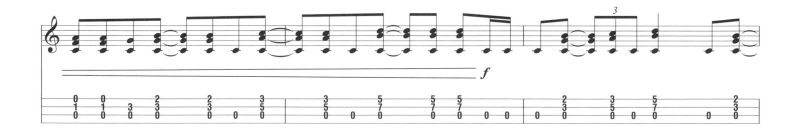

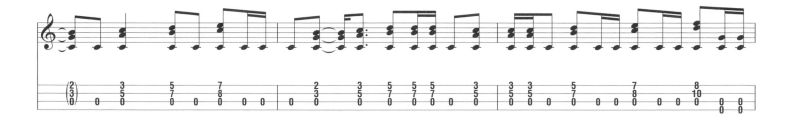

J

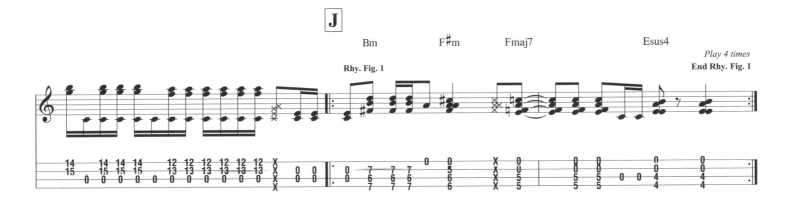

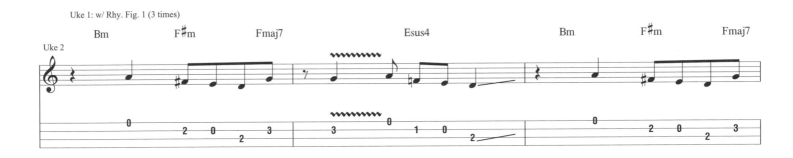

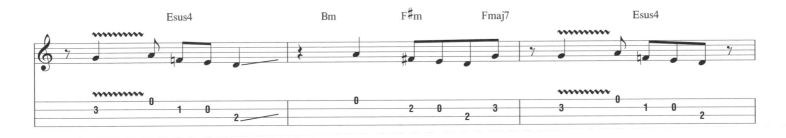

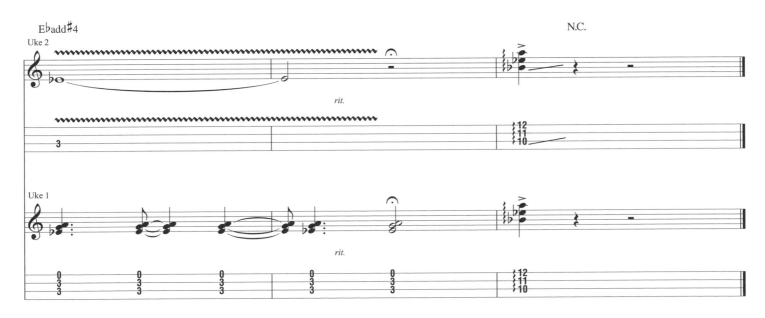

If Six Was Nine

Words and Music by Jimi Hendrix

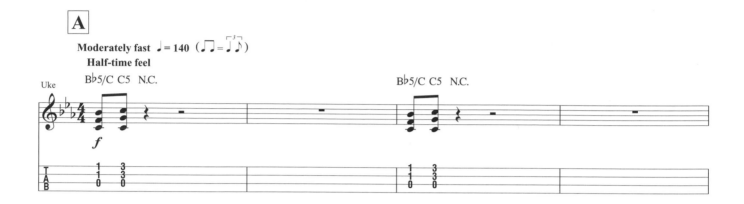

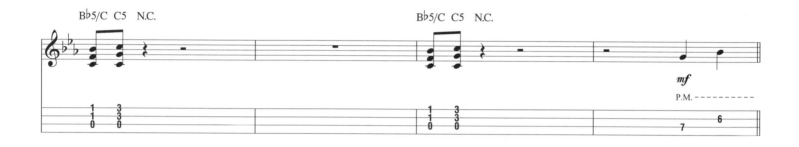

*Chord symbols reflect implied harmony.

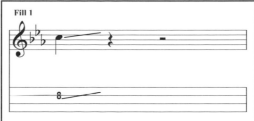

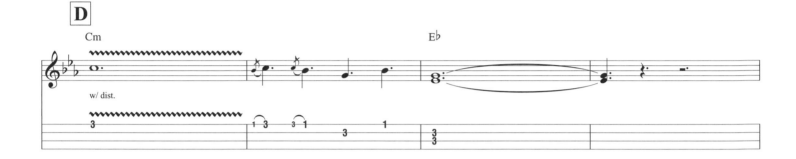

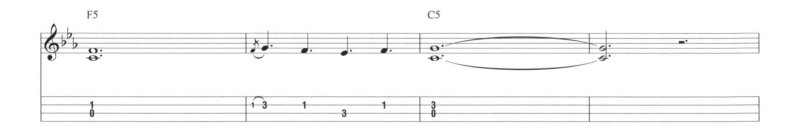

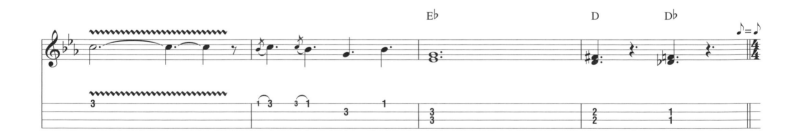

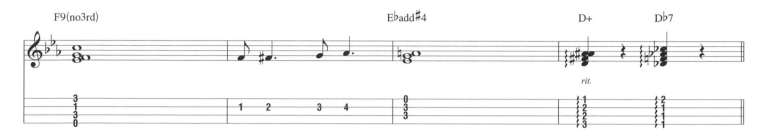

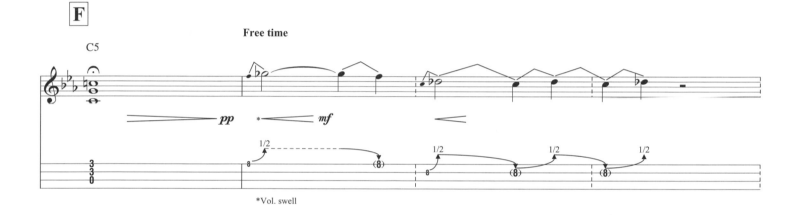

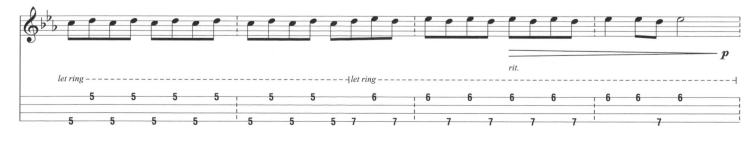

*Decrease/increase tremolo speed w/
decrescendo/crescendo respectively.

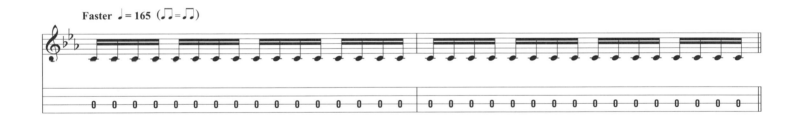

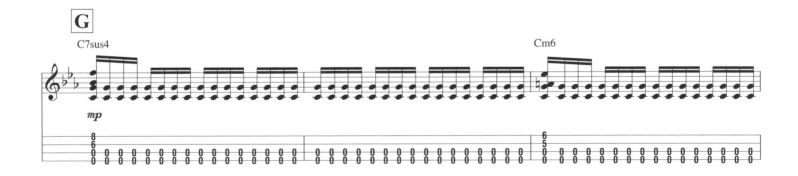

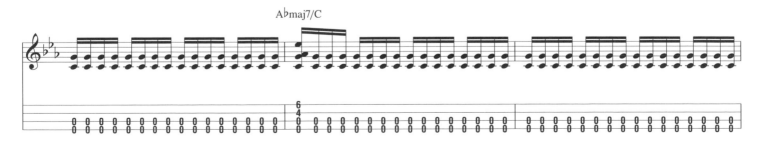

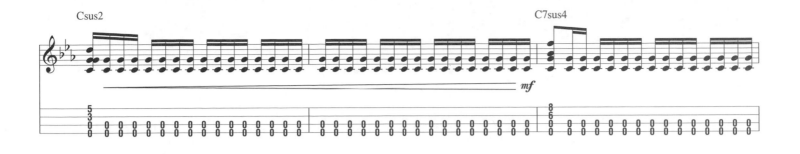

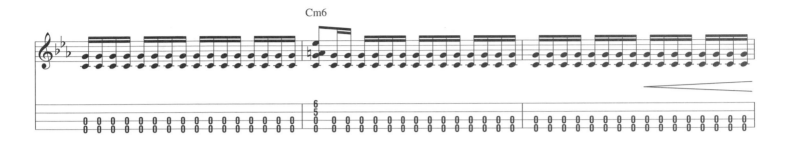

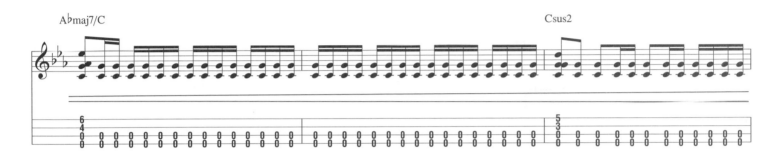

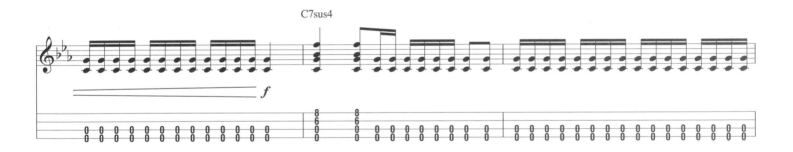

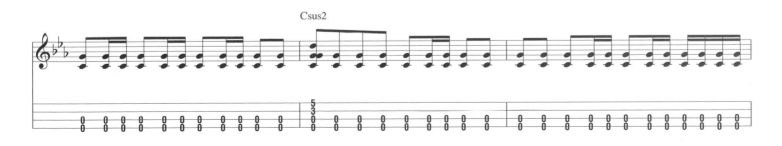

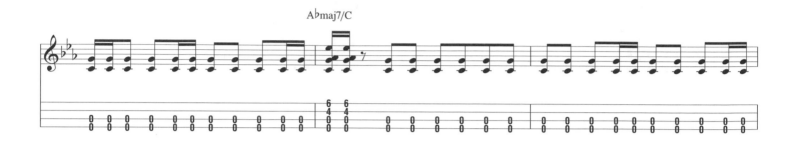

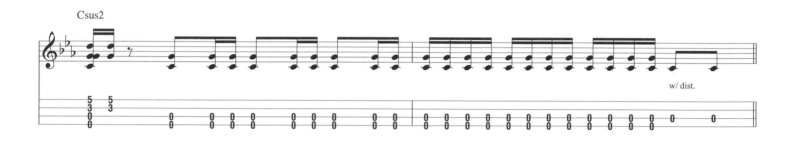

H

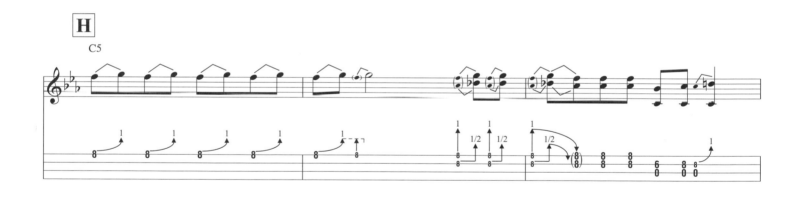

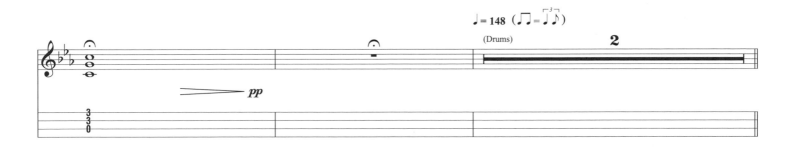

$\quad$ = 148 ($\sqcap$ = $\sqcap$)

(Drums)

2

pp

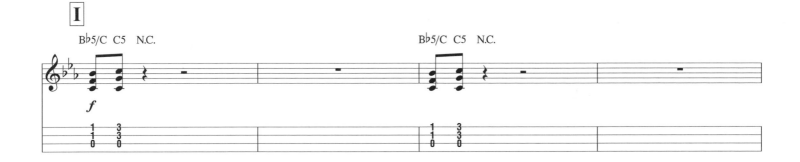

I

B♭5/C C5 N.C.

B♭5/C C5 N.C.

f

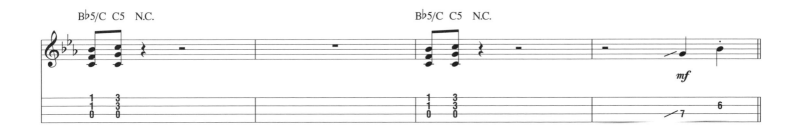

B♭5/C C5 N.C.

B♭5/C C5 N.C.

mf

J

Cm

P.M.

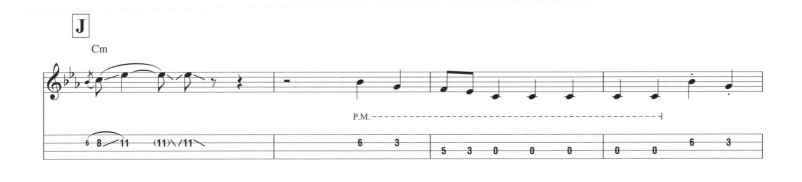

P.M.

P.M.

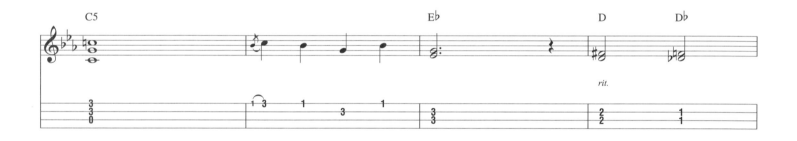

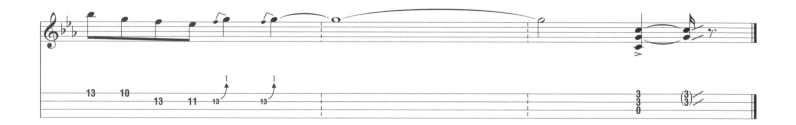

Shape of You

Words and Music by Ed Sheeran, Kevin Briggs, Kandi Burruss, Tameka Cottle, Steve Mac and Johnny McDaid

C

Dm   Gm   Gtr. 2 tacet   A7#9

Oo, wah, oo, wah, oo, wah, oo, wah.   I'm in love with the shape of

F

Uke 3 tacet

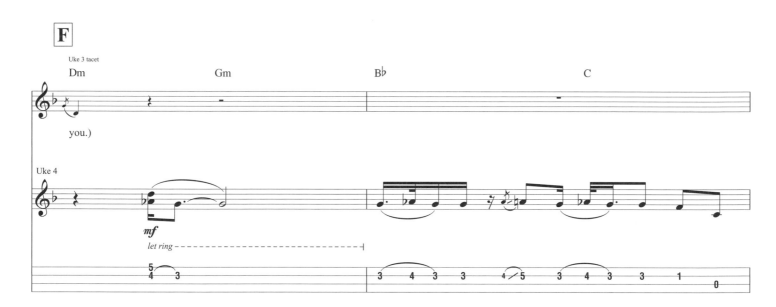

Dm   Gm   B♭   C

you.)

Uke 4

mf

let ring -

Dm   Gm   B♭   C

1/2 hold bend

Go for Broke '18

Written by Jake Shimabukuro

(cont. in slashes)

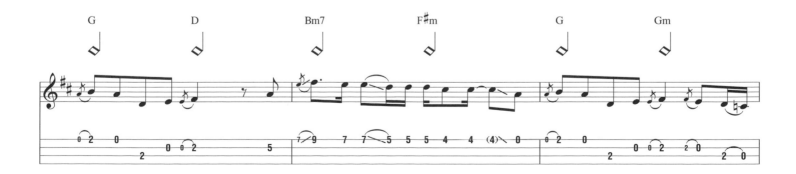

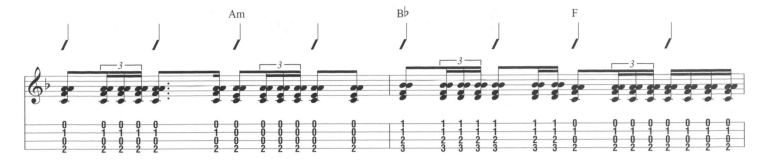

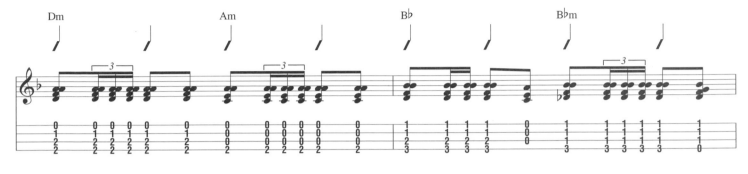

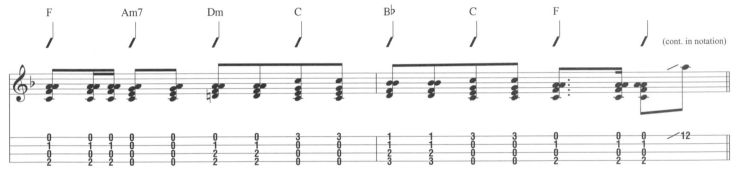

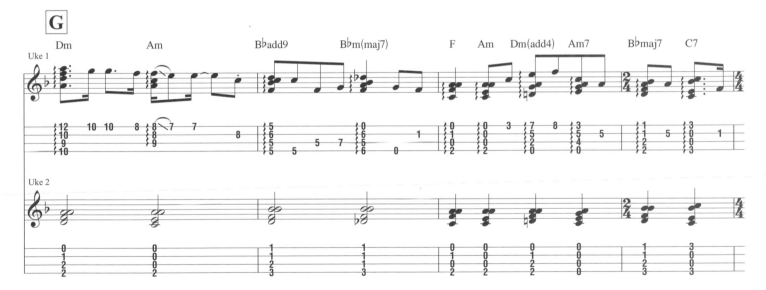

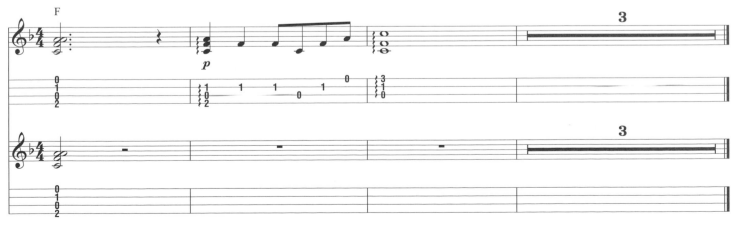

Little Echoes

Written by Jake Shimabukuro

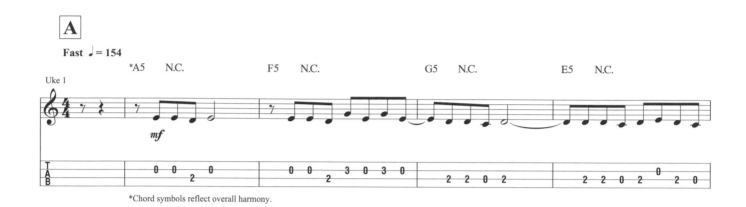

*Chord symbols reflect overall harmony.

**w/ delay

**Set for eighth-note regeneration
w/ multiple decaying repeats.

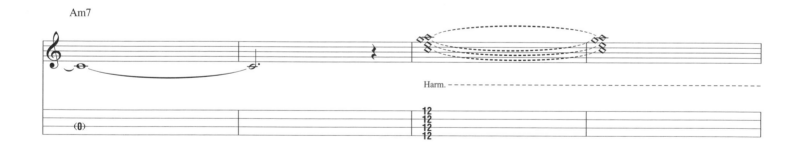

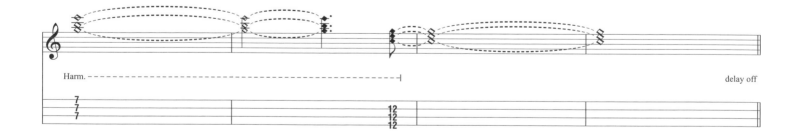

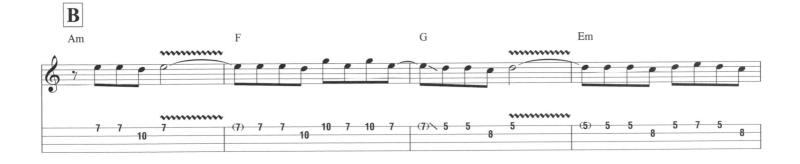

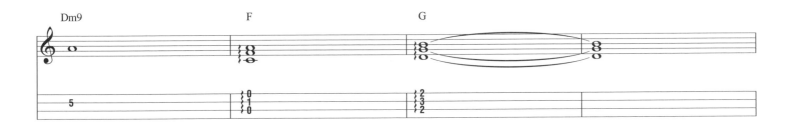

End half-time feel

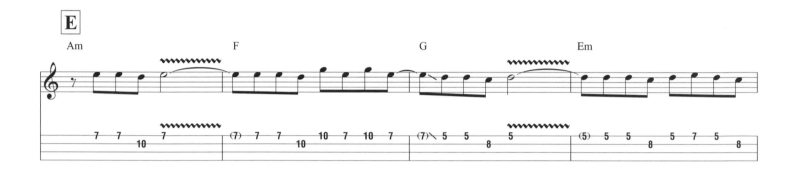

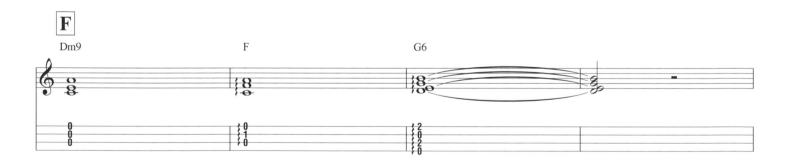

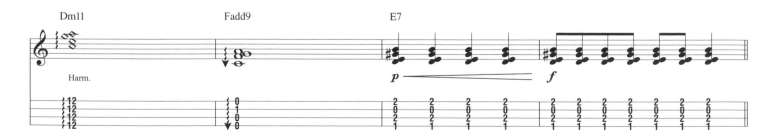

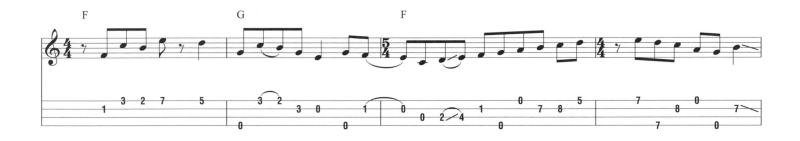

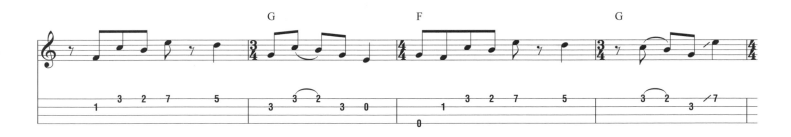

Mahalo John Wayne

Written by Jake Shimabukuro and Brian Shepard

*Chord symbols reflect implied harmony.

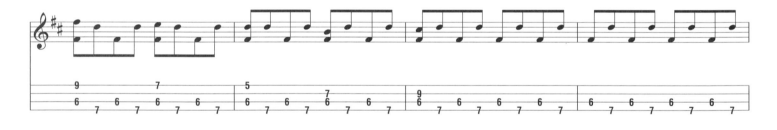

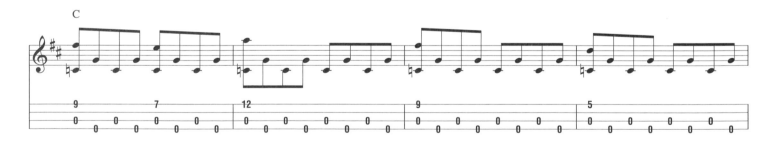

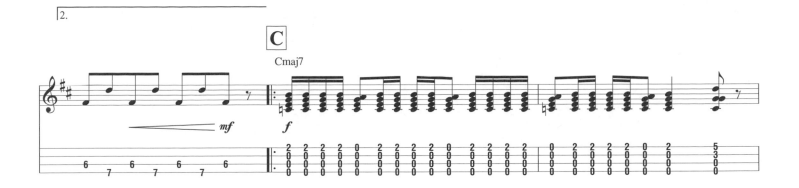

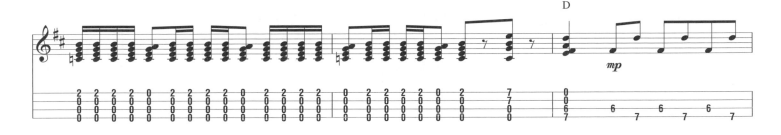

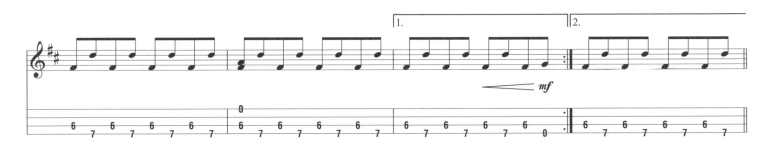

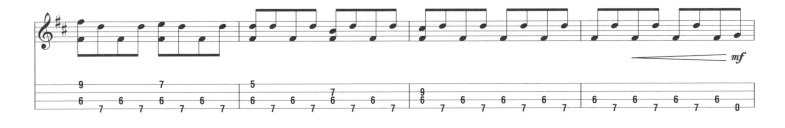

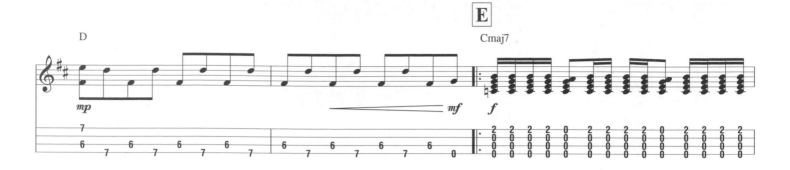

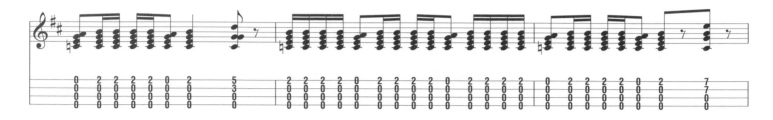

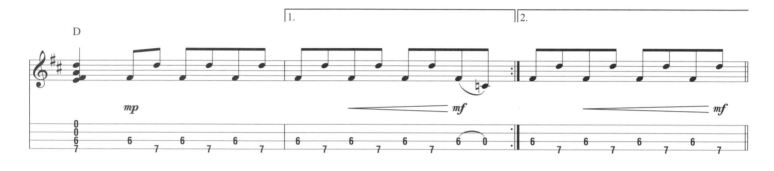

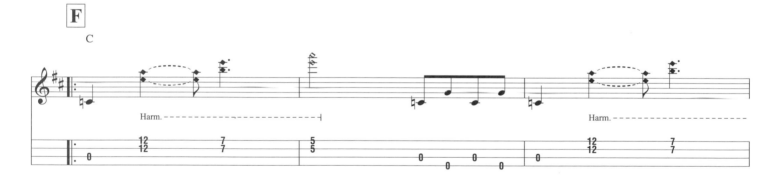

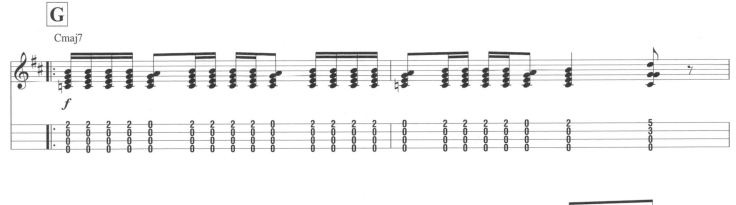

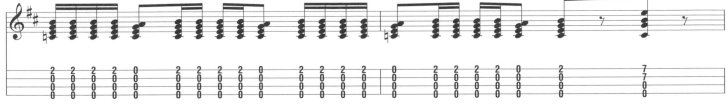

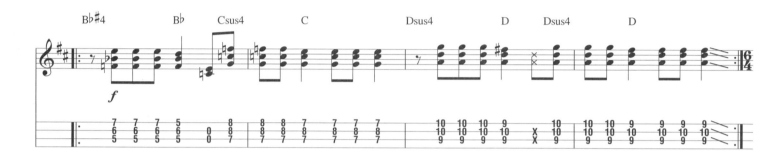

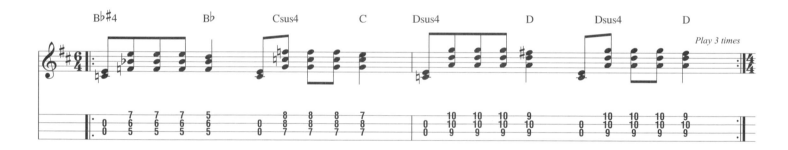

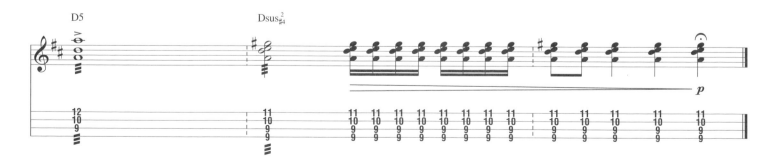

Hallelujah

Words and Music by Leonard Cohen

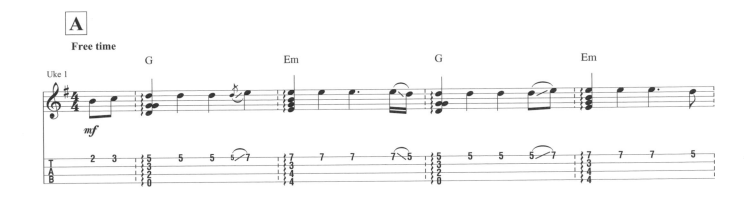

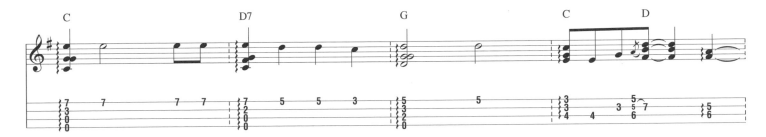

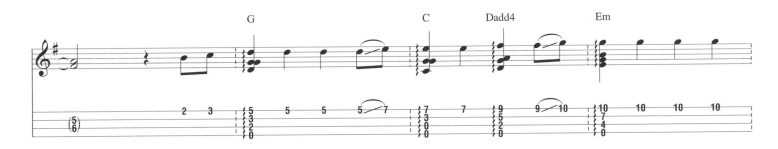

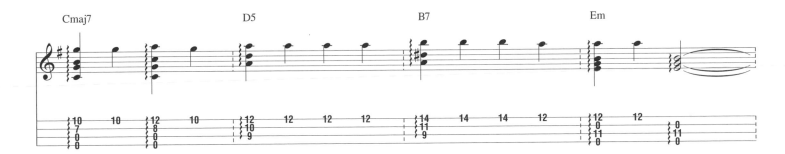

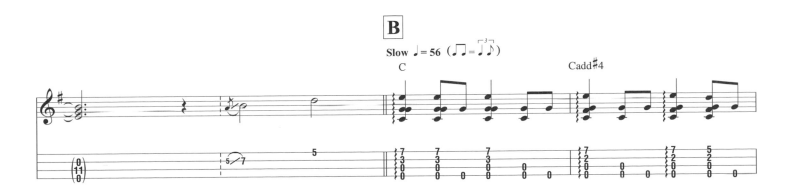

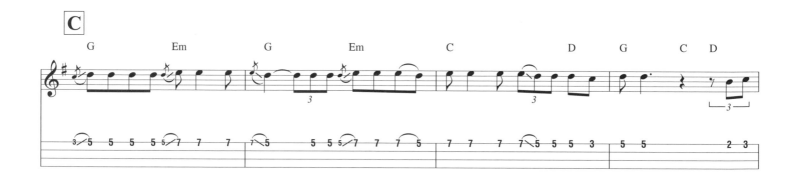

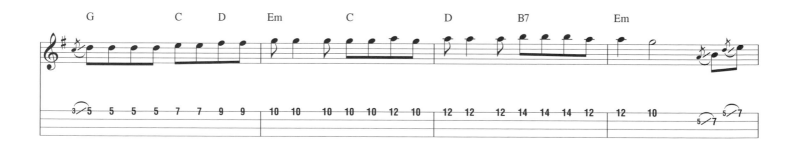

*Played as straight eighth notes.

D

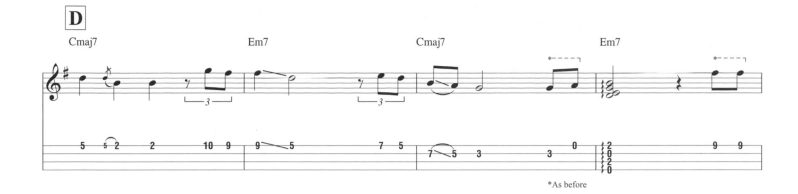

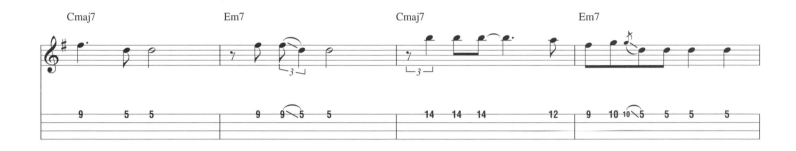

E

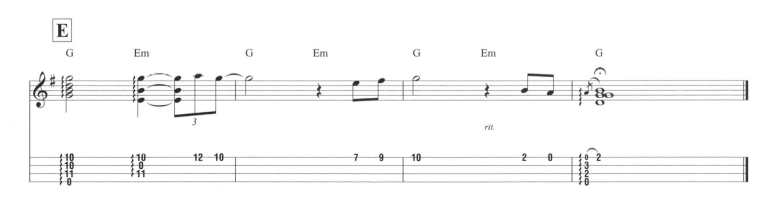

UKULELE NOTATION LEGEND

THE MUSICAL STAFF shows pitches and rhythms and is divided by bar lines into measures. Pitches are named after the first seven letters of the alphabet.

TABLATURE graphically represents the ukulele fingerboard. Each horizontal line represents a a string, and each number represents a fret.

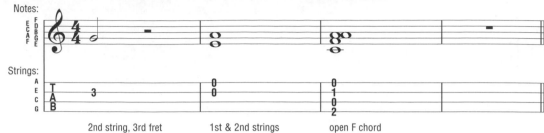

2nd string, 3rd fret

1st & 2nd strings open, played together

open F chord

HALF-STEP BEND: Strike the note and bend up 1/2 step.

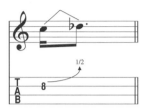

WHOLE-STEP BEND: Strike the note and bend up one step.

GRACE NOTE BEND: Strike the note and immediately bend up as indicated.

SLIGHT (MICROTONE) BEND: Strike the note and bend up 1/4 step.

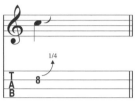

BEND AND RELEASE: Strike the note and bend up as indicated, then release back to the original note. Only the first note is struck.

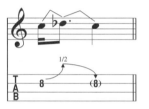

PRE-BEND: Bend the note as indicated, then strike it.

VIBRATO: The string is vibrated by rapidly bending and releasing the note with the fretting hand.

HAMMER-ON: Strike the first (lower) note with one finger, then sound the higher note (on the same string) with another finger by fretting it without picking.

PULL-OFF: Place both fingers on the notes to be sounded. Strike the first note and without picking, pull the finger off to sound the second (lower) note.

LEGATO SLIDE: Strike the first note and then slide the same fret-hand finger up or down to the second note. The second note is not struck.

SHIFT SLIDE: Same as legato slide, except the second note is struck.

TRILL: Very rapidly alternate between the notes indicated by continuously hammering on and pulling off.

TREMOLO PICKING: The note is picked as rapidly and continuously as possible.

NOTE: Tablature numbers in parentheses mean:

1. The note is being sustained over a system (note in standard notation is tied), or

2. The note is sustained, but a new articulation (such as a hammer-on, pull-off, slide or vibrato) begins, or

3. The note is a barely audible "ghost" note (note in standard notation is also in parentheses).

Additional Musical Definitions

 *(accent)* • Accentuate note (play it louder)

 *(staccato)* • Play the note short

D.S. al Coda • Go back to the sign (𝄋), then play until the measure marked "*To Coda*," then skip to the section labelled "**Coda**."

D.C. al Fine • Go back to the beginning of the song and play until the measure marked "*Fine*" (end).

N.C. • No chord.

• Repeat measures between signs.

|1. |2. • When a repeated section has different endings, play the first ending only the first time and the second ending only the second time.